GroupBuilders

50 High-Impact Ideas to Revolutionize Your Adult Ministry

Loveland, Colorado

GroupBuilders: *50 High-Impact Ideas to Revolutionize Your Adult Ministry*
Copyright © 2000 Group Publishing, Inc.

Visit our Web site: *www.grouppublishing.com*

Credits
Contributors: E. Paul Allen, Mikal Keefer, Julie Meiklejohn, Ken Niles, Lori Niles, Pamela J. Shoup, Helen Turnbull, Paul Woods
Editor: Michael D. Warden
Creative Development Editor: Jim Kochenburger
Contributing Editor: John Fanella
Chief Creative Officer: Joani Schultz
Copy Editor: Alison Imbriaco
Art Director: Jenette L. McEntire
Designer: Jenette L. McEntire
Computer Graphic Artist: Fred Schuth
Cover Designer: Liz Howe
Production Manager: Alexander Jorgensen

Library of Congress Cataloging-in-Publication Data
GroupBuilders : 50 high-impact ideas to revolutionize your adult ministry.
    p. cm.
  ISBN 0-7644-2138-7 (alk. paper)
  1. Church group work. 2. Small groups--Religious aspects--Christianity. I. Group Publishing.

BV652.2 .G69 2000
253'.7--dc21
                                                            00-024721

10 9 8 7 6 5 4 3 2 1   09 08 07 06 05 04 03 02 01 00

Contents *3*

Introduction *4*

Introduction

If you're looking for innovative, easy activities to spice up your small group, you've come to the right place. In these pages, you'll find fifty ready-to-go ways to shake up your small-group routine and help group members grow in their faith together.

Before you get into the nitty-gritty of the pages that follow, though, here's a little about the four categories into which this book is divided.

Breaking the Ice • These quick ideas provide great ways for the folks in your small group to get to know one another better. And they're really fun to do! Use these activities anytime you have new people in your group or as a great beginning to one of your small group meetings.

Building Relationships • These creative gems take the notion of "ice-breaker" one step farther, by helping your group members take their friendships to a new level. Through these fun activities your group members will deepen their relationships with one another, build unity, and practice being "the body of Christ" together.

Taking a Fresh Look at Scripture • If you're looking for a fresh, innovative approach to teaching key Bible passages, check these out! Each activity is geared to help group members explore some of the more common Scriptures in some uncommon ways. Don't worry—they're not scary. Just different. Read a few, and you'll see what we mean.

Reaching Out to Others • Building relationships and studying the Bible are key elements in any small group. But no small group is complete if the truths its members learn are never put into practice. These ideas provide the way for your group to do just that. You'll be surprised at how profoundly simple some of the ideas are and how much fun you'll have doing them! Try a few, and your group members will be hooked for life! In the process, they'll learn one of Christianity's most powerful truths: Real joy comes not from serving yourself, but from serving others.

Throughout the book, there are ideas to add extra "wow" and pizazz to the activities. These extra impact ideas are called Wow Tips. Use these creative sugesstions to get the most out of your GroupBuilder activity.

Now, about the variety of ideas within each category: As you know, every small group is different. The people *within* your small group, too, can have vastly different personalities. That's why we've included creative ideas for all sorts of individuals and groups—from the shy and inhibited to the boisterous and bold.

You know your own group's temperament best, so start out by selecting activities that you think people will be comfortable doing. In general, we suggest you keep the risk level low at first. Then, as group members get used to your innovative approach (at this point, they'll start asking questions like, "Where do you get all these creative ideas?" and "Why haven't I ever found a small group like this before?"), begin trying some of the more daring ideas—especially the ones for reaching out to others.

The process for selecting just the right idea for each meeting is simple. Every idea in the book includes a quick overview of the activity and a list of the supplies you'll need. (Most of the activities require only simple supplies that you can find in your home or at your church.) The activities are described as concisely as possible. Scan them quickly to find just the one that fits your needs best.

The main strength of these creative ideas is that they genuinely focus on the three elements that make any small group strong and healthy: Building relationships, studying the Bible, and serving others. We believe you'll be blessed as you experience these activities with your small group. More importantly, we believe that God will be glorified as you use these ideas to help your group members become more mature, committed members of God's family.

WHO AM I?

Overview: People will guess a word and find a partner.

Supplies: You'll need adhesive name tags (or index cards and tape) and markers.

Activity:

Before the meeting, make pairs of name tags for every two people you expect to attend. Think of words that people tend to associate (such as "ball" and "chain"), two words that make another word when combined (such as "over-achiever"), and compound words (such as "junior high"). Write each word on a separate name tag.

Here are a few other suggestions to get your creative juices flowing: dishwasher, vacuum cleaner, moving target, third wheel, drunk driver, and most wanted.

Have group members sit in a circle, then say: **In a moment, I'll put a name tag on your back. A word is printed in the name tag, and it will be your job to determine what that word is. You'll do this by questioning the people around you. You can ask each person only three questions, and all of your questions must have *yes* or *no* answers. For example, you might ask, "Is the word a noun?" or "Is it something that breathes?"**

When you've discovered your secret word, take your name tag off your back and put it on your front. Then you'll need to find your "partner"—the person whose secret word goes best with yours. When you've found your partner, sit down with him or her.

When everyone has identified his or her word and partner, say: **Now I'd like each pair to do two things. First, introduce yourselves to each other, then share your answer to this question:**

- **When have you felt like whatever your name tags describe? Explain.**

For example, if your name tags make the word "overachiever," tell when you have felt like an overachiever and why you felt that way.

After you've responded to that question, I'd like you to work together to figure out three things you have in common. When you're finished, you'll introduce each other to the whole group.

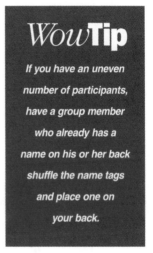

Wow Tip

If you have an uneven number of participants, have a group member who already has a name on his or her back shuffle the name tags and place one on your back.

Give pairs five minutes to complete their assignment. Then have partners introduce each other to the group, telling all that they discovered about their partner through this activity.

A PENNY FOR YOUR THOUGHTS

Overview: Participants will select coins from a bowl and share something significant that happened to them the year the coin was new.

Supplies: You'll need a supply of coins and a bowl.

Activity:

Before group members arrive, select about a dozen coins to place in a bowl. The coins can be pennies, nickels, dimes, or quarters. Be sure the coins represent a range of mint dates so you have some coins from the '90s, '80s, and '70s. Make sure the coins' dates fall within the life span of your group members. As your group arrives, ask participants to toss a few coins into the bowl as well.

Once everyone has arrived, carry the bowl around the room, and have each person select one coin without looking. Making this a "don't look" activity eliminates the tendency for participants to select the shiniest (and, therefore, newest) coins.

After everyone has a coin, say: **Check the date on your coin. What I'd like you to do is think about where you were in life during that year. What**

were you doing? Where were you working? What grade were you in at school? Please share with the group one significant event that happened during that year.

If someone has a coin minted before he or she was born, allow that person to swap for another coin—still without looking.

Some people will claim they can't remember the year or that "nothing happened." Here's where gentle follow-up questions can help evoke a memory from even the blankest minds. Such questions might include:

- Did you have a crush on anyone during that year in school? Who and why?

- Where were you working during that year? What do you remember about working there?

- What was your favorite kind of music during that time of your life? Why?

- Where did you live during that year? What did you like most (or least) about the place?

- Who was in your family at that time? Describe the house where you lived.

Because group members will select the memories they wish to share, they'll reveal only as much as they feel comfortable sharing. Don't probe too vigorously for details—instead, give group members the latitude to stay in their comfort zone.

After the activity, have people toss the coins back in the bowl. Be sure members retrieve any coins they added to the coin supply at the beginning of the activity.

EXTRA CHEESE AND *WHAT?*

Overview: Group members will assemble their perfect pizza and see who shares their tastes.

Supplies: You'll need scissors, paper, pens, and pins.

Activity:

Before group members arrive, cut out a four- or five-inch paper circle for each participant. As group members arrive give each person a circle, a pen, and a pin for attaching the circle to clothing.

On a sheet of paper, list the following menu with the corresponding numbers:

Broccoli	1
Pineapple	2
Extra cheese	3
Sausage	4
Bacon	5
Ham	6
Green peppers	7

Onions	8
Anchovies	9
Sun-dried tomatoes	10

Ask each group member to select up to four favorite toppings and write the numbers on his or her circle. Then, ask group members to find someone whose numbers resemble their own. Perfect matches are not necessary—but may happen!

When your group members have found partners, ask the partners to compare

- favorite radio stations (and why),
- favorite types of soft drink,
- favorite vacation destinations, and
- favorite authors.

Ask pairs to report back to the whole group how closely they matched, then have group members vote to confirm or deny the following claim: **Behavioral scientists believe that people who prefer the same pizza toppings will agree on almost everything else.**

After the vote, ask group members to comment on these questions:

- **Why do you think this claim is true (or untrue)?**
- **What do you think really determines how much people have in common?**
- **What discoveries have you made today that you find encouraging?**

"DOTS" DE WAY IT LOOKS TO ME

Overview: People will work in pairs to draw a figure by connecting a series of dots.

Supplies: You'll need pencils and a copy of the dot grid (p. 30) for every two participants.

Activity:

Have people form pairs. Give each pair a dot grid and two pencils. Tell the pairs that their goal is to work together to create a figure by taking turns connecting dots. The figure must be more than a simple geometric shape. The trick is that partners may not discuss what sort of object they want to create, and they may not speak at any time until the figure is complete.

As partners take turns, they may only add to the figure; they may not erase. When the figure is complete, have partners share what they believe the object is. If they agree, they're finished. If they don't agree about what they have created, they must begin again.

After all groups have completed the activity, ask:

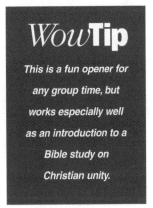

- **How is this game like or unlike trying to act in unity in the church?**

- **What did you learn as you went along?**

- **What do you think would be different if you played again?**

- **How can we learn from our mistakes regarding unity in the church?**

RESTAURANT GUIDE

Overview: Use this activity to quiz group members about local eateries that best "fit the bill" for certain occasions.

Supplies: You'll need newsprint, tape, and a marker.

Activity:

Tape a sheet of newsprint to the wall. Choose a scribe to write participants' responses on the newsprint during this activity. Then say: **If we were describing our town to others, we might take the approach of defining our culture through our local restaurants. We're going to create a restaurant guide, a list of recommendations based on the circumstances surrounding the meal. For example, I might say "This is the place to go after church on Sunday." You'll tell** *the* **place, in your opinion, and why you think it's the perfect spot.**

Choose from the following circumstances, or from your own circumstances, and let people share their perspectives.

Say: **What's the best restaurant to visit when**

- **your wallet is empty?**
- **the gas tank is low?**
- **you really want to impress someone?**
- **you are extra hungry?**
- **you're feeding a family of eight?**
- **you want to take a mini-vacation?**
- **you're celebrating a special event?**
- **you're feeling "daring"?**
- **you want to do a good deed?**
- **you want to experience local flavor?**

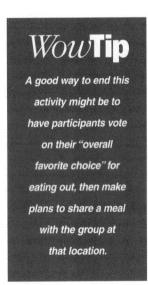

*Wow*Tip

A good way to end this activity might be to have participants vote on their "overall favorite choice" for eating out, then make plans to share a meal with the group at that location.

At the end of the activity, ask:

- **What did you discover about our town through this activity?**
- **What did you discover about one another?**

THINGS I WISH I'D SAID

Overview: Group members will share quotes or proverbs that are particularly meaningful to them.

Supplies: You'll need several books of famous quotes.

Activity:

Once everyone has arrived, say: **We all store up in our minds some pithy sayings that define our perspective on life. I'd like you to share some of your favorite comments on life—quotes or sayings that you really love. Perhaps the source was a bumper sticker, a book of quotes, a poster someone put on a wall during college, or something your great-grandmother used to say.**

After each person has shared, ask people to pair up with the person whose saying most closely parallels his or her own and share how their quotes have affected their lives.

When pairs are finished, bring everyone together, and distribute several books of famous quotes. Have people form groups of three or four, and have groups look through one or more of the books to find a quote that, in some way, communicates their hope for this group. For example, a group might choose a quote about friendship (such as Robert South's quote: "A true friend is the gift of God, and he only who made hearts can unite them.") to show how the group's members hope to build new friendships in the entire group.

Have each group share its quote with the whole group, then use the quotes as the basis for a group prayer. Have group members ask God to make their wishes for the group come true.

*Wow*Tip

This is a good opener to use when you are preparing to study a passage from Proverbs or one of Jesus' sayings.

BREAKING *The* **ICE**

THINK OF ONE...

Overview: Group members will share likes, dislikes, and interests and brainstorm about ideas to explore in future small-group meetings.

Supplies: You'll need newsprint, tape, and a marker.

Activity:

Tape a sheet of newsprint to the wall. Have group members sit in a circle and take turns responding to the following statements. Use as many as you have time for. When you get to the statements on spiritual matters, list participants' responses on a sheet of newsprint. Use these to plan future meeting topics, or choose one to jump in and discuss after the opener.

Say: **Think of one...**

- **way you'd spend your last $10.**

- **food you strongly dislike.**

- **movie you could see again and again.**

- **historical figure you'd like to meet in heaven.**

- **thing you like about yourself.**

- **time God answered your prayers.**

- **struggle you've had with being a Christian.**

- **question you'd like God to answer for you.**

- **Scripture you don't understand.**

- **thing you want to get out of this small group.**

WHO'S INVITED?

Overview: Group members will try to communicate silly situations while at a "party" and discuss how to strengthen communication and unity.

Supplies: You'll need paper and pens.

Activity:

Have people form groups of four. Have each group pick a "party host." Have the party hosts gather in one corner of the room and tell one another their best and worst party experiences. Meanwhile, have the "party goers" secretly work together to come up with a list of biblical characters placed in crazy situations. For example, they might choose:

- Noah in his ark building a roller coaster to pass the time,

- Gideon trying to convince someone to loan him a fleece,

- Joseph presenting his fancy coat to Calvin Klein, or

- David preparing to fight the World Wrestling Federation heavyweight champion.

Once the party goers have come up with enough character situations, assign each character and crazy situation to one of the party goers. Explain that when they join the "party," they must pretend to be their assigned biblical characters engrossed in the crazy situations. However, they cannot say who they are or what they're doing.

When everyone is ready, have the party hosts stand in the center of the room. The party hosts will pretend to receive the party goers in their group.

Have guests arrive at the party one by one, so that the party host can greet each one individually and welcome him or her to the party. As the guests enter, they must act out their biblical characters without directly revealing who they are. They must continue to act out their situations until all the guests have arrived. After all the guests have arrived and are acting out their situations, challenge the party hosts to guess who the guests are and what situations they are acting out. Party hosts may help each other, but may not ask the guests any direct questions. Each guest must continue his or her action until the host guesses the biblical character and the situation. When the hosts have guessed everyone's role and situation, have groups sit together and discuss these questions:

- **If you were the host, how hard was it to guess what situation your guests were in?**

- **If you were a guest, did you make it easy or hard for your host to guess who you were? Explain.**

- **How is this like or unlike meeting someone new?**

- **When you are introduced to a new group of people, do you reveal a lot about yourself, or do you remain quiet? Explain.**

- **When someone new comes to your group, do you try to leave the person alone, or do you ask probing questions?**

After the discussion, say: **It's easy to ignore a new person who may come from a situation that seems "crazy." But we all know what it's like to be on the outside. We're nervous, and we wonder, *Is this group going to like me?* So, as a group member, it's important to identify yourself with people on the outside, especially when you're a disciple of Christ. Think of yourself as someone who *has* to figure out that new person's situation—in order to strengthen the body of Christ. And you may just find a new friend in the process.**

SAY WHAT?

Overview: People will use unusual words to tell something about themselves.

Supplies: You'll need a copy of the "Say What?" handout (p. 31), scissors, and a bowl.

Activity:

Before the activity, cut apart the copy of the "Words and Phrases" handout. Place the "Words and Phrases" slips in a bowl or similar container.

Have everyone sit in a circle. When you're ready to begin, pass the slips around and have each person take one. Tell participants not to tell anyone what's on their slips. Explain that they're to use their words or phrases in sentences that tell something about themselves. Mention that they'll also need to explain why they chose to use the word the way they did. Give participants thirty seconds to think, and then begin. Go around the circle at least once so that each person shares something about himself or herself using the word or phrase on the slip. If you'd like, shuffle and redistribute the slips, then go around another time or two.

WowTip

It's OK if more than one person gets the same word or phrase in this activity. However, if your group is especially large, you may want to add several unusual words and phrases of your own to give the activity more variety. Or you can have the participants form two groups and have them complete the activity separately.

BREAKING *The* ICE

YOU KNOW YOU'LL HAVE A GOOD TIME WHEN...

Overview: Group members will choose objects to represent how their day has gone, think about God's presence in the group, and select objects to represent what they hope to gain from the meeting.

Supplies: You'll need a Bible and a variety of common (or odd) household objects, such as a potato peeler, a bolt, a fork, a ball, a washcloth, a telephone cord, or a pair of pliers. Gather enough items so that you have more items than people in your group.

Activity:

Spread the household items on the floor or on a table where people can see them easily. As people arrive, have each person look at the objects you've gathered and select one to represent what his or her day has been like so far. Then have people sit in a circle and take turns sharing why they chose the object they did.

After all have shared, have group members place the objects back where they found them. Then read aloud Matthew 18:19-20.

After the reading, have participants select objects to represent what they hope to gain from this meeting. Have them share why they chose the objects they did. Then ask:

- **What does this Bible passage say about our time together?**

- **How does it make you feel knowing God is here with us?**

- **How might recognizing God's presence affect your hopes for this meeting?**

TELLING STORIES

Overview: People will summarize favorite childhood stories then guess which story was whose favorite.

Supplies: You'll need index cards and pens.

Activity:

When everyone has arrived, pass out index cards and pens. Have each person summarize his or her favorite childhood story on the card. It can be a Bible story or any other story the participant remembers hearing as a child. Tell people not to put their names on the cards.

After a few minutes, gather the note cards and mix them up. Then read one aloud, and have the group try to guess whose favorite story it was. The person who wrote the story should pretend to guess along with all the others. When the group gets the right answer, have the person explain why that story was his or her favorite. Then read the next card and repeat the pattern.

If your group members are already comfortable with each other, you might want to have some fun discussing the following questions for each story:

- **What does this story reveal about the person whose favorite it was?**

- **How do you think this story has affected the person's life?**

BREAKING *The* ICE

GETTING TO KNOW YOU

Overview: Group members will bring items from home to help people get to know them.

Supplies: Before the meeting, ask each person or couple to bring something from home that represents the person or couple. Have people bring their items in plain brown bags. Tell them they can bring any kind of item and that the items can represent their personalities, lifestyles, work habits, or any other aspect of who they are.

Activity:

As people come in, have them place the objects in the plain brown bags on the table or in another central location. When everyone has arrived, explain that each person will choose a bag, open it, and try to guess who it belongs to. Encourage people to explain their guesses. Then identify who the item belongs to. Ask the item's owner to answer the following questions:

- **Why did you choose this item?**
- **How does this item represent you?**

Allow the selected item's owner to choose the next person to select a bag. Continue the process until all the group members have been identified with their objects. Then ask your group members to work together to recall how each item represented its owner.

Have people form pairs, and ask them to consider how each partner might use his or her item to reach out to others. For example, if someone brought a computer keyboard, he or she might use it to type encouraging letters to others. Give pairs about five minutes to come up with their answers. When time is up, gather everyone together, and have each person share how his or her object can be used to help others.

When the whole group is finished, have group members return to their pairs, and have partners pray for each other, asking God to give them the opportunity to help others this week. After a few minutes, close the prayer time by praying for the entire group.

BREAKING *The* ICE

Dots

Say What?

outrageous

anchovy pizza

Jaguar

Taj Mahal

luge

The Beatles

Gilligan

caramel corn

gorilla

Green Eggs and Ham

mysterious

best friend

roto-tiller

racy

tonsillectomy

extraordinary

Web site

ninety-five miles per hour

embarrassing

James Bond

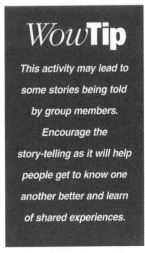

*Wow*Tip

This activity may lead to some stories being told by group members. Encourage the story-telling as it will help people get to know one another better and learn of shared experiences.

BUMPING INTO FRIENDSHIP

Overview: Participants will learn more about one another by asking (and answering) a series of questions.

Supplies: None needed.

Activity:

Before the activity, move furniture so that the center of the room is clear. Have participants spread out and line up along all four walls of the meeting room. Say: **We're going to spend some time getting to know each other better. When I say "go," I'd like you to close your eyes and slowly walk into the center of room. The first person you bump into will be your first partner.**

When people have found partners, say: **Now I'm going to ask a question, and you'll have a few minutes to discuss the answer with your partner.** Ask the first question from the Questions list, and allow a few minutes for partners to discuss it.

Then have participants stand back to back with their partners, close their eyes, and walk slowly away from each other. The first person a participant bumps into is his or her new partner.

Say: **Take a few minutes to discuss the following question with your new partner.** Ask the second question on the list. Continue in this manner until you've used all of the questions. If you'd like, you can add questions of your own.

Questions

- **What was one of the best vacations you've ever been on?**
- **What did you (or do you) like about school?**
- **If you could have dinner with two famous people, who would they be?**
- **Where is your ideal place to live?**
- **What's one thing that makes you angry?**
- **What's a quality you greatly admire in one of your parents?**
- **If Jesus were here on earth today, what do you think would most distress him?**
- **What are two things you would do if you were the leader of your country?**
- **Why do you think people go to church?**

TEAMWORK

Overview: Group members will role play to discover some advantages and pitfalls of working in a small group.

Supplies: You'll need the "Team Roles" handout (p. 60), scissors, envelopes, and a marker.

Activity:

Before the activity, make three (or more) copies of the "Team Roles" handout. You'll want participants to work in clusters of at least three people. If the group consists of six people, make three copies. For seven or eight people, make four copies. Cut apart each handout, and choose roles according to the size of the group. For example, if the group consists of five to eight people, choose two roles. You'll then have six or eight slips of paper. Put each slip in a separate envelope. Separate the envelopes into piles according to roles. (All the "leader" envelopes will be in one pile, for example.) Then write "1" on all the envelopes in one pile, "2" on all the envelopes in another pile, and so on. Finally, shuffle the envelopes.

Have the participants sit in a circle, and say: **I'm going to be giving each of you an envelope. Don't open your envelope until I tell you to.**

Give each participant an envelope, then say: **Now I'd like you to look at the number on your envelope. Take a moment to find the other people with the same number. When you've found them, sit in a circle together.**

Give participants a few moments to do this, then say: **In your envelopes, you'll find instructions for our activity. In a moment, I'd like you to open your envelope and read what's on the paper inside. Don't share what's on your paper with anyone else. When you've finished reading, put your paper back in the envelope, and bring your envelope back to me. When everyone's finished reading, work in your small group to accomplish the task described on your paper. However, you must maintain the character you've been assigned.**

Take the envelopes as participants finish with them, then circulate among the groups, watching and listening.

After about five minutes, ask the groups to stop where they are.

Spend time processing with the group by first asking participants to identify who everyone in the group was. Then lead a discussion of these questions:

- **How did you feel about this activity?**

- **What did this activity teach you about working in groups?**

- **Did you realize that everyone in your group was trying to play the same "role"? Why or why not?**

Review the roles from the handout with the group. Then ask:

- **Which one of these roles do you think you usually play in a group setting?**

- **Which roles are helpful? Which are not?**

SHOPPING SPREE

Overview: Participants will select perfect gifts for each other—without spending a penny.

Supplies: You'll need a stack of catalogs, markers, paper, pens, and a hat.

Activity:

Begin saving catalogs a few weeks before you do this activity so you have a large supply available. If your mailbox isn't routinely stuffed with catalogs (if such a thing is *possible*) set aside advertising pages and inserts from newspapers.

As people in your group arrive, ask them to jot their names on slips of paper. Place the slips in a hat. When everyone has arrived, pass the hat around. Ask each person to pull out a name, but *not* to reveal that name to anyone.

If someone draws his or her own name, return it to the hat and ask the person to draw again.

Announce that people will "buy" a gift for whoever's name appears on the slip of paper they're holding. There's no upper price limit, but the gift *must* be selected from one of the catalogs. The goal is to find a gift that reflects the recipient's interests, talents, or spiritual gifts. For instance, Frank might be given a fishing pole because he enjoys fishing. Bob might get waders because he's a caring person who "wades right in to help anyone in need."

Say: **When you find the perfect gift, circle it and tear out the page. Don't show anyone the gift or the name of the recipient. You'll have five minutes to shop. Go!**

After five minutes, ask each person to share the picture and description of the perfect gift. If you have time, ask your group to guess who the intended recipient might be—and why. If you're short on time, simply let the person who selected the gift explain its significance and present it to the recipient.

As this activity unfolds, pay attention to how on target the gifts are. Listen to the explanations. You'll get valuable feedback about how well your group members really know each other.

BUILDING *Relationships*

TWO-HOUR TRADEOFF

Overview: Participants will exchange two-hour blocks of time to do projects at each others' homes.

Supplies: The person hosting the project will provide needed supplies.

Activity:

When everyone has arrived, say: **There was a time people shared major tasks. Barn raisings. Harvest. Canning. Quilting. It was a tradition for friends and neighbors to take turns helping out with significant jobs. And it seemed the work went more quickly because there was a social aspect to the job. Those days have gone by the wayside—but you're bringing them back!**

We all have projects around the house that we could use some help with—projects that two or more people could do together and visit while they work. During the next few months, let's do "two-hour trade-offs." That is, let's take turns helping each other do some of those jobs that require extra hands.

Ask group members to brainstorm about jobs that fit the following criteria:

- The job can be finished or significantly moved ahead in two hours,

- the job can be done by several people working together,

- people doing the job can chat as they work, and

- the job doesn't require skills *not* found in your potential helpers.

Painting a porch probably qualifies. Hanging dry-wall might qualify. Getting six people together to tune a car won't qualify.

Be aware that not everyone in your group will be able to participate. Not everyone will have an appropriate job to do. Child-care is an issue, as are schedules. For those who can participate, attempt to arrange two-hour swaps between them. The more people participate, the better the chances for relationships to form or strengthen.

*Wow*Tip

A caution: Anyone who receives help needs to be willing to provide an equal amount of hours helping others. It will not *enhance relationships if one individual cajoles other group members into spending an entire weekend finishing off his basement only to then quit the group or be too busy to help anyone else.*

THE SPICE OF LIFE

Overview: Group members will share ideas about how to spice up their spiritual lives.

Supplies: You'll need newsprint, tape, and a marker.

Activity:

Write the word "spice" down the side of a sheet of newsprint, and tape the newsprint to the wall. Ask group members to brainstorm about something that would deepen their relationship with God and that starts with any of the letters in *spice*. They may share either from their own experience or from things they have heard or read. As ideas are presented, write the suggestions beside the letter they begin with.

Here's one group's list of ideas:

S—Spend time in silence, secretly praying about something, then see what God does.

P—Pray "around the clock," talking to God about something that's scheduled for each hour of the day.

I—Insist on a prayer "timeout." Each time a specific key word is mentioned during the day, let it be a reminder to pray about a particular need.

C—Commentaries. Invest in a set, and use it regularly.

E—Enter his gates with thanksgiving instead of a critical spirit.

The acrostic is a great way to get people to start sharing ideas, so don't be rigid about sticking to the letters. Use them as a starting point. After people have completed the acrostic, ask them to share other secrets of a spicy spiritual life.

WowTip

You can use the acrostic strategy to help your group focus on any concept—such as spicing up marriages, family relationships, or the group members' relationships with one another. The rationale is that by limiting options you actually help participants think more deeply about the topic.

SCRAPPIN' WITH THE SCRIPTURE

Overview: Group members will document their responses to Scripture for posterity.

Supplies: You'll need an instant-print camera, film, scrapbook paper, scissors, a glue stick, and a fine-point marker.

Activity:

This activity is particularly effective when group members delve into a Scripture that's especially difficult to understand or to implement in their lives. As you introduce the Scripture to your group, tell group members they're going to use facial expressions (instead of words) to communicate their initial reaction to the Scripture. For example, if the Bible passage is confusing, a group member might try to look confused. Or if the passage makes group members angry, they might scrunch up their faces in a scowl.

Read the Bible passage a few times to make sure everyone has a chance to absorb what it's saying. Then use an instant-print camera to take a group photograph of group members expressing their reaction to the Scripture with their faces.

When the picture develops, pass it around the group, and have each person explain his or her expression. Afterward, dive into the study.

At the end of the study of that Bible passage, have group members stage another photograph to follow up the first one. In this photograph, have group members use facial expressions to communicate how they feel about the Bible passage now. When the photograph develops, pass it around the group and have each person explain how (or whether) his or her expression changed from the first photograph to the second.

Make a scrapbook page that chronicles the experience. Glue the photos on the page, label them "Before" and "After," and write the Scripture passage you studied. Then use the photographs to launch a more personal discussion of how a particular Scripture passage affects group members in different ways. Allow time for group members to share their own perspectives and struggles with the difficult Bible passage you studied.

WowTip

Make color copies of the scrapbook page so each member can keep a lasting reminder of the experience. Also, you may wish to chronicle many of your group experiences in a scrapbook format and keep them in a permanent album as a way to affirm the significance of your time spent together.

BUILDING *Relationships*

WowTip

If you're looking for a few difficult or controversial Bible passages to study, try these: Deuteronomy 20:10-18; Ecclesiastes 1:1-2; Hosea 1:2-3; Matthew 10:37-39; and 1 Corinthians 14:33b-35.

COMEDY CLUB

Overview: Group members will share a comic strip that reveals something about themselves.

Supplies: You'll need scissors, tape, and the comic strip section from several days of newspapers.

Activity:

As group members arrive, give them each a comic strip section from a recent edition of the newspaper. It's OK if some group members get the same comic strips, but try to include comic strip sections from several days' (or weeks') worth of newspapers.

Tell group members to read through the comics and each choose one cartoon that illustrates or re-minds them of something that has happened to them recently. When all the group members have chosen cartoons, have them cut the cartoons out. Then have group members take turns sharing their cartoon and explaining how it relates to a recent event in their own lives.

Next, have group members return to their comic strip sections and find the cartoon characters they believe are most like them. These pictures should also be cut out. Then have group members take turns sharing their cartoon character and ex-plaining why they think that character is most like them.

After everyone shares, distribute tape, and have each group member tape the cartoon character to his or her chest and keep it on for the rest of the meeting.

WowTip

To build relationships over time, have your group decide on a comic strip in the local paper that has a theme of interest to all of them. Some possibilities are listed below: Calvin and Hobbes, For Better or Worse, *and* Family Cir-cus *would work well for young families.* Dilbert *and* Cathy *would work well for groups of college or career* people. Peanuts, B.C., *and* The Wizard of Id *would work well in mixed groups.* Your group's interests will determine the best comic strip. Each week, have group members bring their favorite comic strip of that week and explain why they liked it. Over time, this will help group members learn about one another's sense of humor and way of looking at the world.

BUILDING Relationships

HOME-SPUD TALES

Overview: Group members will share potato-bar toppings based on child-hood experiences.

Supplies: You'll need one baked potato for each group member. You'll also need plates, forks, knives, spoons, and napkins.

Activity:

Before the meeting, ask your group members to come hungry and to bring a potato topping that reminds them of their childhood in some way. It might be a favorite family food, something that was served on specific occasions, or something that reminds them of their relationships with parents or siblings. For example, a member might bring mixed veggies for relationships that were "all mixed up." Someone else might bring butter to represent parents who seemed to "grease" the way for him or her.

When the group arrives, have everyone serve themselves from the variety of options. As you eat together, have people explain the significance of what they brought. Ask:

- **How does the memory you shared about your family affect your day-to-day life now?**

- **What steps are you taking to pass this on—or not pass it on—to others?**

- **In what ways has your relationship with your family shaped your relationship with God? with other people?**

PURPOSE STATEMENTS

Overview: Group members will attempt to formulate a purpose statement for the group.

Supplies: You'll need newsprint, tape, marker, paper, and pencils.

Activity:

Many group members will have participated in the process of developing a mission statement. This activity, which is based on the same process, allows the group to form a purpose statement describing its "mission." The statement shouldn't simply combine all contributions. Instead, the group should attempt to synthesize the underlying essence of its response into one unified statement.

Here's a brief outline of the steps your group might pursue to develop its purpose statement:

Step 1: *Think about it.* Allow about one minute for silent reflection.

Step 2: *Discuss in pairs.* Have group members form pairs to discuss their thoughts about this question: What should be the purpose of this group?

Step 3: *Write on.* Distribute paper and pencils, and have each person write a purpose statement for the group.

Step 4: *Read out.* Have each person read his or her statement aloud; ask others not to comment.

Step 5: *Discuss as a group.* Help group members discuss the individual statements and look for underlying principles and similarities. Write key ideas on newsprint taped to the wall.

Step 6: *Propose synthesis statements.* Have individuals propose statements that pull the core thoughts together.

Step 7: *Refine and define.* Encourage people to reword the proposals until the group reaches a consensus.

Once the summary statement is complete, say: **While our individual responses to our group's purpose may be unique, we can learn a lot through the process of seeking unity. We don't use this process to silence individuality, but to create unity in purpose and direction.**

Close the activity by reading aloud Philippians 2:1-4.

BURSTING BUBBLES

Overview: Group members will share what they wish they were, discuss good things they've discovered about themselves, and encourage one another about who they are.

Supplies: You'll need a balloon for each person, markers, and a pin.

Activity:

Give everyone a balloon and make available a variety of markers. Have group members draw or write on their balloons something they wish they were but are not. Allow a few minutes for people to write or draw. Then have each person share what he or she drew or wrote and explain why. After each person has shared, talk about how we sometimes overlook the good things about ourselves while looking only at the things we wish we could change. Ask:

- **When was a time someone told you something good about yourself that you didn't even realize?**

- **How did it feel to realize that about yourself?**

- **What does it do to us when we dwell only on things we wish we could be?**

After your discussion, take the pin. Turn to the person next to you, pop his or her balloon, and say: **Sorry to burst your bubble. You may not be** [what the person put on his or her balloon], **but you certainly are** [something you like about the person]. Then give that person the pin and continue in the same pattern around the room until every balloon has been popped and every person has been encouraged.

STONE SOUP

Overview: Group members will bring items to contribute to soup that all will share, and they will compare contributing to the soup with contributing to your group.

Supplies: You'll need a large pot, water, salt and pepper, a stove for cooking, table utensils, bread and cheese (to accompany the soup), and drinks.

Activity:

The meeting before you want to do this activity, read the classic "Stone Soup" story (p. 53) aloud to your group. Then tell each person to bring something to your next meeting to contribute to "stone" soup.

Before your meeting, get water started in a pot, but be sure to leave room for things to be added. As people arrive, add their ingredients to the pot, and add salt and pepper to taste.

Allow the soup to simmer during your meeting, then serve it early enough to allow time for you to read the "Stone Soup" story again and have the group discuss the following questions:

- **How is what we did in making the soup like what the soldiers and villagers did in the story?**

- **What did your personal contribution add to the soup?** (Have everyone answer.)

- **How is what we did in contributing to the soup similar to what we do in contributing to this group?**

Stone Soup

Three soldiers trudged down a road in a remote part of the country. Besides being tired, they had eaten almost nothing for two days.

"How I would like a good dinner tonight," said the first.

"And a bed to sleep in," added the second.

"But that is impossible," said the third.

On they marched, until they saw the lights of a village. "Maybe we'll find a bite to eat and a bed to sleep in," they thought.

The people of the town feared soldiers, some of whom had treated them harshly. When they heard that three soldiers were coming down the road, they whispered, "Soldiers are always hungry. And the harvest was so poor that we have little for ourselves." So they hurried to hide their food. They hid barley in hay lofts, carrots under quilts, and buckets of milk down the wells. They hid all they had to eat. Then they waited.

The soldiers stopped at the first house. "Good evening to you," they said. "Could you spare a bit of food for three hungry soldiers?"

"We have no food for ourselves," the residents said.

The soldiers went to the next house. "Could you spare a bit of food?" they asked. "And do you have a corner where we could sleep for the night?"

"Oh, no," the man said. "We gave all we could spare to the soldiers who came before you."

"And our beds are full," said the woman.

(Continued on p. 61)

TO TELL THE TRUTH

Overview: In this adaptation of the old TV game show, *To Tell the Truth,* group members will pretend to be another group member and help the rest of the group get to know that person.

Supplies: None needed.

Activity:

Have people form clusters of three or four. Within each cluster, have the person newest to the group be "the subject." Each of the other cluster members should then ask "the subject" lots of questions to learn about him or her. Give clusters five to ten minutes for this questioning.

WowTip

Don't use this activity to introduce new people. They could feel uneasy or even that the activity is making fun of them.

Then the cluster members (except "the subject") will become "contestants." Have the contestants from the first cluster stand up before the whole group and say, "My name is..." and finish the sentence with the name of their subject. Then allow about five minutes for group members to ask the contestants questions about their subject (who the contestants claim to be). Advise the contestants that, if they don't know an answer, they should fake it. A lot of laughs will likely be the result.

When you call time, have the real "subject" stand and select which of the contestants best portrayed him or her, then correct any answers that the contestants faked. Repeat the activity for other clusters.

You might want to do this activity regularly as part of your meeting until every person has had a chance to be a "subject."

BUILDING *Relationships*

PICTURE JOURNEYS

Overview: People will learn more about each other's lives by creating stories with pictures.

Supplies: You'll need index cards and markers. Before the activity, you'll need to ask each person to bring as many photos as possible from different times and events in their lives. Pictures should include any or all of the following: babyhood, elementary age, teenage years, early adulthood, marriage, career, and vacations. Encourage group members to bring enough pictures to give an overview of their lives.

Activity:

Before participants arrive, set out the index cards and markers. When everyone has arrived, ask group members to take one marker and an index card for each picture they brought. Make sure they write their name on the back of each card.

Have group members each find a partner whom they don't know well. Have group members give their pictures and cards to their partners—without explaining the pictures. Then encourage each partner to use the pictures to create a wild story describing the other person's life. To help organize their thoughts, partners may use the index cards to write notes to accompany each photograph. After about ten minutes, have everyone come back together and form a circle.

Give each person about two to three minutes to share a story about his or her partner's life, using the photographs and index cards. Encourage people to have fun with their stories by fabricating crazy events whenever possible.

After each person shares, have the partner retell the story, correcting any embellishments or mistakes his or her partner may have made.

Conclude by congratulating group members on their creativity and their interesting lives. Then say: **All of our lives are made up of wonderful stories. And even though it was fun to hear all the embellishments, it's even more fun to share the real stories of our lives. As we walk together on this journey, make sure to share your story with others. Not only will your stories help us grow closer together, they will often inspire us to grow closer to God.**

BUILDING *Relationships*

STAR GAZING

Overview: Participants will interview partners who are pretending to be famous, then discuss how to use the talents they have.

Supplies: You'll need notepads, pencils, snacks, soft drinks, newsprint, marker, and tape.

Activity:

Before everyone arrives, set out snacks and soft drinks. Write these questions on a sheet of newsprint, and tape it to the wall:

How did you know you had this particular talent?

How many years did it take to become famous?

What's the most difficult thing about being famous?

What's the best thing about being famous?

How would you encourage someone else who shares your talent?

As participants arrive, invite them to enjoy the snacks and take time for conversation.

After participants have had time to enjoy the treats, bring everyone together in a circle. Give each person a notepad and pencil, and have people form pairs. Have one person in each pair pretend to be a reporter. The other person gets to be famous. Have group members choose their own reason to be famous. It can be something they already do or something they'd like to do.

Have the reporters use the questions on the newsprint to interview their famous person. Tell them they have about ten minutes to ask their questions.

After ten minutes have partners switch roles. They can ask the same questions and add others if they wish. When the interviews are over, bring everyone back together as a group. If time permits, give everyone a chance to share his or her questions and answers. If not, choose two or three people to share their interviews with the rest of the group.

When they finish sharing, have participants re-form their pairs. Tell partners to discuss these questions:

- **What talent(s) do you have today?**

- **How can you use that talent to build relationships with others?**

- **How can you bring them closer to God using your talent?**

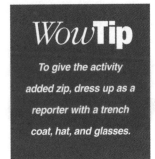

WowTip

To give the activity added zip, dress up as a reporter with a trench coat, hat, and glasses.

Give each person about five minutes to ask and answer the questions.

After everyone has had a chance to share, lead the group in the following prayer: **Dear God, thank you for giving me this talent. Help me use it for your glory. Give me ideas on how to use this talent to show others how to know you better. Allow me to use this talent to grow closer to someone this week. In Jesus' name, amen.**

Team Roles

You play the **leader** of the group. You're excited and ready to go! You want the members of your group to get along well with each other and develop good relationships within the group. The purpose of your meeting is to help the participants decide on a group mission project (such as painting a house or doing a car wash). You start the meeting when you sense the others are ready.

You play a **follower**. Choose one person in the group and go along with whatever he or she says. The purpose of the meeting is to decide on a group mission project; you don't seem to have many opinions in the matter.

You play a **hyperactive overachiever**. You have too much energy and have a hard time sitting still. You're anxious about your position with the others in the group, and you really want your idea to be the one that is used. The purpose of the meeting is to decide on a group mission project, but you're having a hard time paying attention.

You play a **naysayer**. Whatever others seem to be enthusiastic about, you'll find something wrong with it or a reason it can't be done. The purpose of the meeting is to decide on a group mission project. You really don't like any of the ideas presented, but you don't really have a better idea.

You play a **shy person**. You don't like to draw attention to yourself. People need to coax a lot out of you. The purpose of the meeting is to decide on a group mission project. You don't seem to have much of an opinion.

Stone Soup *(continued from p. 53)*

At each house, the response was the same: no one had food or a place for the soldiers to stay. The people had very good reasons, such as feeding the sick and the children. The villagers stood in the street and sighed, acting as hungry as they could.

Standing in the middle of the town, the first soldier called out, "Good people! We are three hungry soldiers in a strange land. Since your tired fields have left you nothing to share, we will help you make soup from stones."

Soon the town's largest pot was placed over a fire and filled half full of water. Then the soldiers dropped in three smooth stones. "Now this will be a fine soup, " said one soldier, "but any soup needs salt and pepper." One villager conceded that she could bring some salt and pepper and went to fetch it.

"Stones make good soup, but carrots would make it so much better," the second soldier added.

A woman said, "Why, I think I have a carrot or two!" Soon she was cutting up several carrots into the pot.

As the kettle boiled on, the villagers found more and more to contribute. Soon barley, cabbage, beef, and potatoes had made their way into the kettle.

Tables and torches were set up in the square, and soon all sat down to eat. One villager said, "Such a great soup would be better with bread and cider," and brought forth the last two. Never had the village seen such a feast. Never had the villagers tasted such delicious soup. They ate and drank and danced well into the night, and the soldiers slept well in the nicest beds in town.

As the three prepared to leave the next day, the villagers handed them a satchel of homemade breads and cheese for their trip, thankful for the lesson the soldiers had taught them.

UNPACK YOUR BAGS

Overview: Use this activity to help participants make following Jesus their top priority.

Supplies: You'll need a Bible, a large backpack, a portable CD or cassette player, a watch, a map, a small teddy bear, a small mirror, a dollar bill, a ball of string, scissors, a calculator, index cards, pens, and tape.

Activity:

Before the activity, write each of the following prayers on an index card and tape it to the appropriate item. Then put the items in the backpack.

- "Lord, help us tune out the many distractions in our lives and find a quiet place to listen to you." (Tape the card to the portable CD or cassette player.)

- "Lord, help us slow down. Teach us how to make time for you." (Tape the card to the watch.)

- "Lord, help us accept your plans for our lives instead of telling you where we want to go." (Tape the card to the map.)

- "Lord, help us look inside each person for you instead of focusing only on appearances." (Tape the card to the mirror.)

- "Lord, give us the courage to set aside our insecurities and be willing to take risks in order to follow you." (Tape the card to the teddy bear.)

- "Lord, help us realize that the things of real value are not measured by how much they cost." (Tape the card to the dollar bill.)

- "Lord, help us set aside any grudges that tangle up our hearts. Show us that you are the tie that binds." (Tape the card to the ball of string.)

- "Lord, help us cut out our bad habits and learn how to depend only on you." (Tape the card to the scissors.)

- "Lord, help us not to put facts and figures before faith. Teach us to believe even when we cannot see. (Tape the card to the calculator.)

Have participants sit in a circle. Say: **We're going to take a closer look at our priorities in life and at what Jesus wants our priorities to be. I'm going to begin by reading a story from Jesus' life that's probably familiar to you. As I read, I'd like you to put yourself in the young man's shoes and imagine what your response to Jesus might have been.**

Read Mark 10:17-27 aloud. Then ask:

- **How do you think you would have responded in this situation?**

- **What kinds of things would be difficult for you to give up in order to follow Jesus?**

Give everyone an index card and a pen. Say: **I'm going to pass around a backpack full of things which may sometimes hold us back in our journey with Jesus. Please take one item from the backpack and hold onto it.** Pass around the backpack. If there are more items than people, give some people more than one item. If you have more participants than items, have people pair up or form trios to draw items from the backpack.

Say: **Now, in an attitude of prayer, let's take turns sharing what's written on the cards taped to our items. As you listen to others' prayers, think about what it might mean for you to let go of each item.** Have participants read their prayers, one at a time. When they're finished, say: **Please continue this prayer for yourself by writing on your index card one thing you'd like to "unpack" to help you travel more closely with Jesus.**

Give participants a few moments to write and then say: **Now I'll pass the backpack around again. Please put both your item and your index card in the backpack. As you do so, commit in your heart to leaving those things behind.**

ASK FOR INSIGHT

Overview: Group members will use an acrostic to work through a Bible passage.

Supplies: You'll need Bibles with concordances, newsprint, a marker, tape, paper, and pens.

Activity:

On a piece of newsprint, write

   A—Analyze and associate

   S—Surrender

   K—Know

Then tape the newsprint to a wall.

Have group members take paper and pens and find partners. Then explain how to use the acrostic.

Say: **A stands for *analyze* and *associate*. Read the scripture passage, and pull out the main ideas. You can also break the passage down into smaller parts. Once you have done this, use a concordance to associate** the main ideas with other passages to get a more global perspective of what the Bible says about each component of the passage. Use any other Bible tools that would help your intellectual understanding of the passage.

S stands for *surrender.* Look at what the passage says, and ask yourself, "Is there anything in this passage that goes 'against my grain'? Why does it bother me? What part of my perspective would need to change to bring my life into harmony with this passage? How can my behavior better reflect the message of this passage?" Pray about the answers to these questions, asking the Holy Spirit to make the changes necessary to model the message of this passage in daily life.

K stands for *know.* What should I know after interacting with this passage? Is there a part of this passage I'd like to commit to memory? What do I know about myself that I didn't know before grappling with this passage? What do I need to take action on in regard to this passage?

After pairs have worked through this process, have them regroup and share insights about both the passage and the process.

The ASK plan for study ensures a personal connection to the passage and helps individuals move from the cognitive to the emotive impact of God's word.

TAKING A *Fresh* LOOK AT *Scripture*

ANALOGY WALK

Overview: Group members will take a walk through the neighborhood, creating analogies and parables about the kingdom of God.

Supplies: You'll need at least three Bibles.

Activity:

Once your group has arrived, say: **Throughout the Gospels, Jesus uses analogies to help his audience understand the kingdom of God. By comparing the kingdom to a mustard seed, yeast, hidden treasure, or a man sowing seed, Jesus highlights a truth about the kingdom of God.**

We're going to do the same. On a walk through the neighborhood, let's see if we can make analogies that reveal truths about the kingdom of God.

For instance, we might see a sprinkler watering a lawn and say the kingdom of God is like a sprinkler, because God's Word brings new life to what it touches. Or as we walk under a tree we might say, "The kingdom of God is like the branches of a tree, because it shelters us."

Walk as a group through your neighborhood, pausing to pray for the people who live on the streets. Let what you see prompt analogies, and encourage people to think of as many as possible.

When you return to your group's meeting place, ask volunteers to read these passages aloud: Matthew 13:24-30; 13:31-32; 13:33-35. Ask group members to comment on how these parables have helped them understand the nature of God's kingdom.

TAKING A *Fresh* **LOOK AT** *Scripture*

WAY LEADS TO WAY

Overview: Group members will use their imaginations to project logical consequences to scriptural obedience.

Supplies: You'll need Bibles.

Activity:

When everyone has arrived, lead participants through a study of John 13:1-16. For example, you might begin with a simple foot-washing service, then guide participants to examine why Jesus washed his disciples' feet, and what he was trying to teach them (and us).

At the end of the study, ask one group member this question:

> • **If you habitually obeyed what Jesus commands in this passage, what might happen?**

Ask the next person in the group,

> • **What might happen then?**

Continue around the group, asking each person to project a potential outcome of the previous person's contribution.

Using this strategy, it's easy to see how applying the Word of God can really change the world.

WowTip

This simple method of real-life application can be used for any Bible passage that focuses on what Christians should believe or do. Here are some other Scriptures that work well with this approach:

• Luke 9:23-27

• Luke 12:22-24

• Romans 12:9-16

• Ephesians 4:29-32

TAKING A *Fresh* LOOK AT *Scripture*

IT'S QUESTIONABLE

Overview: Group members will ask open-ended questions for discussion of the passage they are studying.

Supplies: You'll need Bibles, paper, and a pencil for each person.

Activity:

Instead of being the one with all the questions, give group members the opportunity to ask their own questions to spark additional discussion of a passage after the basic truths have been discussed.

To help keep these questions open-ended, assign the following question starters to specific people:

- How might...?

- Why would...?

- How did...?

- Why is...?

- Where can...?

- What would...?

- Who might...?

- When could...?

- How would...?

As each participant poses a question, allow others to respond. Great Bible passages to study with this activity include: Galatians 5:22-23; Ephesians 3:14-19; Philippians 2:1-4; Colossians 3:1-10; 1 Thessalonians 5:16-22; James 1:1-8; and 2 Peter 1:3-11.

While you may lose the sense of being in control of the discussion, the potential benefits of encouraging this kind of input from participants are great. You can rely on the Holy Spirit's wisdom to help you direct the discussion to its greatest level of productivity.

TAKING A *Fresh* **LOOK AT** *Scripture*

FLIP

Overview: Group members begin a discussion about sin by attempting to avoid saying certain numbers as the whole group counts in succession.

Supplies: You'll need a Bible.

Activity:

This variation of the old party game Buzz can help lead into a discussion of sin based on 1 Corinthians 10:12-13.

After reading the passage, begin the activity by having the group count, with each person saying the next number. Explain that, beginning with ten, every number that is divisible by three or that contains a three must be replaced with *flip*. For example, "ten, eleven, *flip*, one-*flip*, fourteen, *flip*, sixteen, seventeen, *flip*, nineteen, twenty, *flip*, twenty-two, twenty-*flip*," In the first round, when a player misses a *flip*, he or she is out.

In the second round, encourage players to find ways to warn people as they approach a *flip* number. For example, players might wink or snap their fingers to warn others of an upcoming *flip*. After both rounds, ask the following questions:

- **How did you feel about round one?**

- **How was the experience of round two different for you?**

Then ask:

- **Coming to a number that had to be replaced by flip was both predictable and inevitable. How is that like or unlike temptation in our lives?**

- **How was round two like or unlike your experience of the support of the body of Christ in relation to temptation and sin?**

Continue the study, delving into the aspects of temptation and sin your Bible passage leads you to think about.

CURRENT EVENTS, TIMELESS ANSWERS

Overview: Group members will examine current events, then explore what the Bible has to say about those issues.

Supplies: You'll need news clippings of current events and Bibles with indexes or concordances.

Activity:

Bring in several news clippings about current events on social issues. If your group has more than five or six people, you may want to break into two or more groups for discussion. Let groups choose the event they'd like to explore, perhaps by a show of hands. Have someone read the news item aloud and begin the discussion with these questions:

- **What is the major issue or debate here?**

- **What do you believe about this issue?**

- **What do you think is the majority opinion in the country about this issue?**

- **What does the Bible say about this issue?**

Allow participants time to look up Scriptures that address the issue and share what they find. Encourage a lively debate, but limit time on responses if someone starts to monopolize the discussion.

Some topics that might provide good discussion are: cloning, same-sex marriage, war or violence, immoral or dishonest activity of public officials, or current issues within your denomination or churches in general.

TAKING A *Fresh* LOOK AT *Scripture*

PRINCIPLES FOR A CHRISTLIKE HOUSEHOLD

Overview: Participants will use Scripture to explore the basis for a happy
Christian home.

Supplies: You'll need Bibles, and photocopies of the "Principles for a
Christlike Household" handout (p. 88).

Activity:

Say: **Christian fellowship begins at home with one's own family. A strong, happy family, living by Christian principles, provides children with a solid foundation for life and provides adults with a model for behavior at home, at work, and in the community.**

Distribute the "Principles for a Christlike Household" handout. Review the list, and have group members share family situations in which these principles might apply. If you have single adults in your group, have them relate the principles to their immediate families, who are not necessarily living in their households.

Then discuss these questions:

- **How might you share these principles with your family?**

- **What are some ways you can get your family to refer to these often and put them into practice?**

- **What's one principle you'll try to put into practice immediately?**

Encourage group members to post these principles in their homes and incorporate them into their daily lives. Suggest that people add to the list as the family members find appropriate Scripture. A family might also make a photocopy of the principles, cut the copy so that each principle is on a strip, and have family members draw a principle each week to put into practice for that week.

TAKING A *Fresh* **LOOK AT** *Scripture*

STRESSBUSTER

Overview: In this activity, participants will look at sources of stresses in their lives and ways to alleviate that stress with prayer and fellowship.

Supplies: You'll need Bibles, modeling dough or beanbags, a cassette or CD of relaxing music, and a cassette or CD player.

Activity:

Adults always have some sort of stress in their lives, whether it's jobs, children, aging parents, finances, addictions, temptations, or just the day-to-day busyness of life. This activity will give them the opportunity to share those issues and look at how prayer and fellowship can help them cope.

Gather group members in a circle, and give each one a small handful of modeling dough or a squishy beanbag. Tell people to squeeze the modeling dough or beanbag as a stress reliever as they take turns sharing one or two sources of stress in their lives. Give everyone an opportunity to share in as much detail as you have time for.

Then ask:

- **Is squeezing this object helping to relieve your stress? Explain why or why not.**

Then take a few minutes to play some relaxing music. Tell participants to relax, close their eyes, and think good thoughts to banish the stress. Ask:

- **Did the music help relieve your stress? Why or why not?** After you have a few answers, continue:

There are many other stress relievers available to us in the form of massage (no, the masseuse is not coming in next!), exercise, even medication. But I think the best stressbusters of all are prayer, Scripture study, and the fellowship of Christian friends. Let's explore some stressbuster Scriptures that you can turn to when you really need strength.

Have group members take turns reading these Scriptures, or as many as you have time for. After each Scripture is read, lead a short discussion on how that Scripture can help relieve or cope with stress.

- Philippians 4:13
- 1 Corinthians 10:13
- Matthew 11:28-30
- Matthew 7:7-8
- 2 Corinthians 1:3-11
- 2 Corinthians 12:7-10
- Psalm 86
- Psalm 62

Read aloud Galatians 6:2, then close in prayer, having group members take turns praying aloud if they feel comfortable doing this. Ask your group to commit to praying for one another all week. When the group meets next, take an update on the status of stress!

TAKING A *Fresh* LOOK AT *Scripture*

LINKING PRAYERS

Overview: Group members will pray in an unusual way, then explore how the Bible tells us to pray.

Supplies: You'll need Bibles.

Activity:

Begin by having everyone sit in a circle. Say: **Let's pray together. However, we're going to pray in an unusual manner. Everyone will contribute one word at a time to our prayer as we go around the circle. No fair saying "amen" until we've gone around at least twice!**

Have the person on your left start the prayer with one word and continue around the circle making up a group prayer before someone ends with "amen." It's OK if this exercise produces laughter, awkward pauses, or a very odd prayer. Afterward ask:

• **Did it feel as if we were saying a sincere prayer? Why or why not?**

• **Do you think God prefers a certain type of prayer? Explain.**

• **What kinds of obstacles or distractions in your life keep you from praying as you would like to? from praying with others?**

Have adults find partners and have each pair read and discuss one of the following Scriptures and themes. If you have more pairs than Scriptures, assign the same Scripture to two or more pairs.

- Pray continually and give thanks always (1 Thessalonians 5:17-18).

- God knows the intent of our prayers through the Holy Spirit (Romans 8:26-27).

- Pray at every opportunity (Ephesians 6:18).

- Pray alone; God anticipates our needs (Matthew 6:5-8).

- Real prayer begins with the heart rather than the mouth (Isaiah 29:13).

- Praise the Lord at all times (Psalm 34:1).

Gather everyone together again, and have pairs briefly share their Scriptures and discussions. Group members may want to share how they have made time for prayer in their lives, how to keep a prayer journal, or other methods that allow and encourage them to pray regularly despite daily distractions.

Close this activity with another circle prayer. This time have people take turns around the circle adding a phrase, such as a special prayer request or words of praise and thanks.

WowTip

Not everyone feels comfortable praying aloud, but shared prayer is a great way for your small-group members to grow closer to one another as they share prayer requests and praises. This activity provides an unusual way to help group members pray aloud together and learn how God wants us to pray.

TAKING A *Fresh* LOOK AT *Scripture*

SING IT!

Overview: Group members will perform songs based on the Psalms, and discuss how praise offered to God can take many different forms and styles.

Supplies: You'll need Bibles, paper, pens, and two paper lunch bags.

Activity:

Before class, write (or type) the following psalms on separate sheets of paper: Psalms 1; 8; 11; 14; 19; 23; 32; 37; 74; 89; and 104. Place these slips in one of the paper bags.

Then write the following types of music on separate sheets of paper: blues, opera, marching band music, rap, rock, disco, commercial jingle, country, gospel, oldies rock, and Gregorian chant. Place these slips in the other paper bag.

Have your class form groups of four or fewer and tell each group it's going to put one of the Psalms to music. Allow each group to choose one psalm and one type of music by drawing one slip from each of the paper bags. Then give the groups about ten minutes to create a short song that fits the psalm and the musical style they chose. Be sure each group member contributes to writing the song.

If your groups have trouble creating their songs, offer these suggestions:

- They don't have to include every line from their psalms in their songs. Even just two lines of a psalm can make an entire song.

- They can think of popular songs from the musical styles they chose and simply rewrite that song with the words from the psalms.

- Ensure the groups they can have fun and be silly, as long as the messages of their songs reflect the messages of the psalms they chose.

When groups have finished their songs, allow them to perform their songs for the rest of the class. Then have groups discuss these questions:

- **How hard was it to write your psalm in a specific style of music? Explain.**

- **Do you think the musical style your group selected is an appropriate style for a psalm? Why or why not?**

- **How effective do you think the musical style your group selected would be in relaying a message to someone who likes the psalms?**

- **How effective do you think the psalm your group selected would be to someone who likes or recognizes that musical style?**

- **Which is more important to the audience: the musical style or the message? Explain.**

Say: **We know how important the message of God's Word is. And the beauty of God's Word is that it can reach *anybody,* no matter what that person's tastes or experiences. And we can reach out to God, no matter what our personal tastes or experiences. Our praises don't have to be particularly harmonious, and they don't have to fit a certain genre. It's good enough to God that our praises come from the heart, no matter what the style.**

Close by singing a well-known song of praise, such as "Awesome God" or "How Majestic Is Your Name."

MORE HONORABLE

Overview: Group members will read and discuss a passage of Scripture, then write titles they'd like for biographies of their lives.

Supplies: You'll need Bibles, pens, and index cards.

Activity:

Begin this activity by having someone read aloud 1 Chronicles 4:1-10. Have others follow along in their Bibles. Then ask:

- **Who stood out in this reading?**

- **Why was Jabez singled out in the midst of this genealogy?**

- **Why do you think God granted Jabez' request?**

Say: **A good title for a biography of Jabez' life might have been** *More Honorable Than His Brothers.*

Give each group member a pen and an index card. Have your group members write the title they'd like for their biographies after they're gone.

When everyone has written a title, have group members share what they've written and why. Then discuss:

- **What can we each do to make sure our biography title comes true?**

- **What role does God play in our reaching that goal?**

Then ask group members to write their response to the following question on their index cards:

- **What commitment are you willing to make so that this title will come true?**

Encourage group members to post their biography titles (and their commitments) at home to remind them of Jabez and of what they want to be remembered for.

FIRST-CENTURY CHRISTIANITY REVISITED

Overview: In this activity, group members will examine a sample of first-century Christianity to discover what they can learn from it to become better twenty-first century Christians.

Supplies: You'll need Bibles, pens, and paper.

Activity:

Begin by discussing the following question:

- **What would it mean to be a first-century-type Christian today?**

After a few minutes of discussion, have people read together Acts 2:42-47. Then form teams of three and make sure each team has at least one Bible. Have teams rewrite this passage as if they were telling a story that was happening in today's culture. If you have poetically- or musically-inclined groups, they may want to put their presentation into a poem or set it to the tune of a familiar song. Give groups at least fifteen minutes to discuss the passage and come up with their rewritten version, then have all groups present what they've written. After the presentation, discuss:

- **What were the differences in our stories?**

- **What were the similarities?**

- **Which story seemed most realistic?**

- **How were the stories similar to what we do in our group? How were they different?**

- **What might we learn from this passage to make our group more effective?**

- **What might we learn from this passage to help us be better twenty-first-century Christians?**

TAKING A *Fresh* LOOK AT *Scripture*

Principles for a Christlike Household

1. "Love one another" (from John 13:34).

2. "Serve one another in love" (Galatians 5:13b).

3. "Be devoted to one another in brotherly love. Honor one another above yourselves" (Romans 12:10).

4. "Carry each other's burdens" (Galatians 6:2a).

5. "Confess your sins to each other and pray for each other so that you may be healed" (James 5:16a).

6. "Be kind and compassionate to one another, forgiving each other, just as in Christ God forgave you" (Ephesians 4:32).

7. "Let the word of Christ dwell in you richly as you teach and admonish one another with all wisdom, and as you sing psalms, hymns and spiritual songs with gratitude in your hearts to God" (Colossians 3:16).

8. "Rejoice with those who rejoice; mourn with those who mourn. Live in harmony with one another" (Romans 12:15-16a).

9. "Encourage one another and build each other up" (1 Thessalonians 5:11a).

10. "Whatever you do, work at it with all your heart, as working for the Lord, not for men" (Colossians 3:23).

BLOOD BROTHERS

Overview: The group will visit a community blood center or church blood drive to donate blood.

Supplies: You'll need transportation for the group.

Activity:

Donating blood is safe and quick, and it meets a very real human need. Unfortunately, less than six percent of North Americans donate blood even once per year.

Call your local blood center and see what convenient donation opportunities exist in your area. Coordinate with your small group, then make reservations so your group doesn't need to wait in line.

It's important to note that not everyone can or should give blood. And some of your group members may have a complete aversion to all things medical.

So be gracious in letting people off the hook—but keep them involved. Ask those not giving blood to be drivers, or to bring gourmet cookies and fresh orange juice to serve the blood donors in your group. One small group of non-donors volunteered to serve as "encouragers" at a community blood drive. They served cookies to donors and thanked people who gave blood.

REACHING *Out* TO *Others*

POUNDING WITH A PURPOSE

Overview: Group members will provide practical support and encouragement for your pastor.

Supplies: You'll need markers, index cards, tape, and transportation for the group.

Activity:

Many rural churches once had a tradition of "poundings." Each church family brought a pound of food to stock the pastor's pantry.

The tradition has fallen out of favor, and many pastors were grateful to see it go. Generally speaking, they'd rather be paid in cash than in lentils and beans. And how many cans of spinach does one pastor need?

With this activity you'll revive the tradition—and add a pastor-pleasing twist.

In preparation for this activity, ask group members to bring five dollars to give away. Then, as a group, visit a local supermarket. Your goal: Each member of your group will buy an item (no more than a pound) that somehow reflects an affirmation for your pastor. For instance, someone might purchase a pound of hamburger because your pastor's sermons are "meaty." A bag of sugar might land in the basket because the pastor has a "sweet spirit." As your group wanders the aisles, talk about what's right with your pastor. Let it be a time of prayerful support.

When you've checked out of the supermarket (split the cost of the food or let everyone pay for his or her own item), go somewhere so that people can jot down on an index card what their items symbolize. Have people tape the cards to the items. Then have them either place the items in a bag for later delivery to the pastor or take the items directly to the pastor so they can deliver the affirmations in person.

COOKIE PATROL

Overview: The group will encourage police officers by delivering cookies to the station house.

Supplies: You'll need to ask each participant to prepare a dozen home-made cookies for this event. You'll also need transportation.

Activity:

Many law enforcement officers begin to wonder if anyone appreciates their role in the community. Their more memorable encounters with the public, as they enforce laws and investigate crimes, are often negative. They see the worst of human nature.

Your group will reach out and serve this group of public servants with an encouraging visit.

Call your community police station and speak with the chief or another administrative officer. Explain that your group appreciates the police officers and would like to thank them for a job well done by dropping off snacks the officers on duty can enjoy. Don't be put off if your motives or the safety of the cookies are questioned; police departments by necessity must be concerned about security issues. If a group member or your pastor has a friend who works as an officer, make initial contact through that individual.

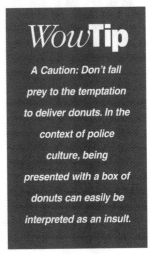

WowTip

A Caution: Don't fall prey to the temptation to deliver donuts. In the context of police culture, being presented with a box of donuts can easily be interpreted as an insult.

If possible, visit the station when many officers will be on-site—for example, at a shift change or at periodic meetings. Ask for the opportunity for your group to say a thirty-second thank-you, applaud the efforts of the men and women who are present, and then leave quickly. Police officers are busy people.

Your impact can be tremendous. Most career police officers can count on one hand the number of times a citizen's group has said "thank you."

REACHING *Out* TO *Others*

T.A.P. INTO YOUTH

Overview: Group members will "adopt" young people in an effort to offer support.

Supplies: You'll need journals and pens.

Activity:

Research from the Search Institute tells us that, in order for young people to grow up healthy, competent, and caring, they must possess certain "developmental assets." Many of these assets are internal traits, but some are assets that come from the outside. One asset is relationships with adults who are *not* their parents. In fact, Search Institute's research indicates that youth need special support from *at least* three adults outside their immediate family.

In order to T.A.P. into youth, members of your group need to commit to the following steps:

1. taking an interest;

2. asking direct, specific, and informed questions; and

3. praying on a regular basis.

Ask your church's youth sponsor to recommend several young people whose parents are not part of your small group (one for every two people in your small group), or have partners in the group select a teenager they're already acquainted with. It's great if the partners can be two men or two women, who will be adopting youth of the same sex. Provide a journal and pen for each pair. Then give pairs these directions:

T—*Taking an interest.* **Find out a little about the teenager you're adopting. You can do this by asking the young person directly, explaining your interest in supporting him or her with prayer, interviewing the parents (with the youth's permission), and observing. You may wish to invite the youth out for ice cream or dinner, with parental permission. Use the journal to take notes. This shouldn't be a one shot thing. It should be a process that helps you begin to really get to know the world of the youth you're adopting. As you discover areas of interest, you may wish to do simple things to help connect in specific arenas. For example, if you discover a teenager is struggling with a math class and one of you sees a cartoon about math, clip it out and give it to the young person. It's a simple way to let that teenager know this interest surpasses an "assignment."**

A—*Asking direct, specific, and informed questions.* **At least once a week, seek out the young person to ask how things are going, either in person, by phone, or by e-mail. Rather than asking a general question, ask specifically about something the teenager has mentioned. Asking doesn't need to be a long and drawn out check-in. It's simply a way to be consistent in showing the young person that someone is in his or her corner.**

P—*Praying regularly.* **At prayer time during your small group meeting, pair up for three to five minutes of prayer specifically for the youth. Record prayer topics and results in the journal.**

This formula for T.A.P.-ping into youth is only a beginning. Ask the Holy Spirit to reveal ways to expand the investment in the youth each pair adopts. Some "adoptions" will require very little investment for a very high impact in the student's life. Other pairs may invest quite a bit and see very little response from the youth. Consistency is key. This is more than a one-time outreach project. It is a chance to make a real and lasting difference in the life of one specific individual.

POP-TOP PARTY

Overview: Group members will creatively contribute to a shelter or food distribution center.

Supplies: You'll need a pop-up tent or trailer and one or more of the following snack foods: popcorn, Pop-Tarts pastries, Pop Rocks candy, and soda pop.

Activity:

In preparation for this activity's kickoff, announce that you'll meet in a special place. Ask your group to bring in some things for a shelter or food pantry that can be given to someone and eaten on the spur of the moment. Each item must have a "pop-top" ring. Some items they might consider include individual tuna cans, snack-size fruit or pudding, sardines, Vienna sausages, or fruit juice. Give prizes for the most creative and the most yummy.

Conduct your meeting in a pop-up tent or trailer, and serve one or more of the suggested snacks.

After the kickoff, continue this unusual food drive for several weeks, allowing group members to share any prize finds they come up with in subsequent weeks. Deliver the canned goods to a service organization that specializes in working with transients.

REACHING *Out* TO *Others*

TREAT OR TRICK

Overview: Group members will knock on doors, *giving* a treat rather than getting one.

Supplies: You'll need many rolls of Life Savers candy, tape, and cards preprinted with the words "Come meet the real Life Saver—Jesus Christ" and the name and service times of your church or information about your group.

Activity:

Do this activity sometime before October 31, as your neighborhood is antici-pating giving candy to children. Prepare the preprinted cards by taping the wrapped candy on.

On the designated day, you may wish to have your group dress in Bible char-acter costumes. Explain to the group that they'll be offering a reverse "Trick or Treat" to people who live near your church or small group meeting place. Your group members may want to spend several minutes developing a "script" to use as they meet the neighbors. Agree on a time and location to regroup. Then canvass the neighborhood in pairs, knocking on doors and giving the treats to those you visit.

When your group reassembles, ask:

- **What was the biggest surprise to you about your experience?**

- **How did people seem to respond to your message?**

- **What would you have liked to have been different about your ex-perience?**

- **Who impressed you as a person you could share more deeply with?**

- **What ways do you feel you could follow up this experience?**

REACHING *Out* TO *Others*

PROJECT PRAYER

Overview: Group members will learn how prayer can be a powerful act of service.

Supplies: You'll need a Bible, pens, and journals or paper.

Activity:

Allow each person in your group time to write in a journal. Guide class members as they write by giving these instructions: **Think about a group of people who have extended an act of service to your community. You might write about teachers, policemen, volunteers, pastors, or social workers. How has this group of people changed the lives of others? Has this group of people ever affected your life personally? Explain. Write about some concerns or trials this group might face on a daily basis. Describe some specific examples of service performed by a member of this group.**

After members have written for two to three minutes, have the class form pairs or trios and discuss these questions:

- **Why did you focus your writing on the group you chose?**

- **How has the group you chose had an impact on others' lives?**

- **What kind of trials do you think these people face?**

- **How can you help support these people in their acts of service?**

Explain that supporting people who have dedicated time to service of others can be a very important mission project itself. Also explain that while many people think missions work is something done in the community or overseas, it can also take place privately, in the form of prayer.

Have the pairs or trios take time to pray—silently or otherwise—for each group they've mentioned. They can ask God to give these groups guidance and strength, and they can praise God for the love he has shared through the efforts of these people.

After each group has spent time in prayer, ask members to write in their journals again. Guide them as they write by saying: **Think about something that weighs heavy on your heart right now. Perhaps you're having a conflict with someone, or maybe you're facing pain or stress. Does how you react to this problem affect your relationship with family or friends? How has this problem affected your spiritual life? How can you change the focus of this problem into an opportunity to serve others?**

Explain that using prayer as a means of missions work is not only a way to support others, it also helps us focus on serving others in our private lives. Encourage groups to commit for the next few weeks to this prayer service project. Say: **Each time the personal problem you wrote about comes into your mind, take time to focus in prayer on ways you can personally serve others in an effort to mend broken relationships or help those you know who are struggling. Then pray again for the people in your community who have devoted themselves to serving others. Ask God to show you how you can help them do their jobs more effectively.**

Read aloud Galatians 6:2. Encourage class members to follow up with progress reports on how focusing their prayers on others might have helped alleviate burdens in their own lives.

STORY TIME

Overview: Participants will write and design children's books to read to preschool and kindergarten classes.

Supplies: You'll need Bibles, paper, pencils, construction paper or poster board, yarn, a hole punch, and colorful markers.

Activity:

Have people form groups of three or four, and give each group a Bible. Tell the groups that they're going to write a children's book based on a biblical truth. Allow the groups five or six minutes to come to an agreement as to which biblical truth they'd like to convey to kids.

Then have groups write and draw a picture book for preschool or kindergarten-age children. Encourage groups to try different approaches to making the biblical truths more fun or more real for kids. For example, they might create a story with forest animals as the main characters to illustrate John 13:34. Or they might retell one of Jesus' parables with imaginary creatures as the main characters.

You might want to encourage each group member's active participation by assigning responsibilities. Two people can write the story, one person can draw the pictures, and a fourth person can color the pictures.

Or try this fun twist: Time the groups in ten-minute intervals. For the first ten minutes, each group will write a story. Then groups will trade stories. For the next ten minutes, the groups will contribute art to the stories they received in the trade. Groups will then trade books for a third time. For the final ten minutes, groups will contribute color to the pages and bind the books together.

Tell your groups to make a six- to ten-page storybook. Be sure participants design a cover and list each group member as a contributing author. Show them how to bind books by punching three holes near the edge, threading the yarn through the holes and tying the yarn.

When all groups have finished designing their books, make plans to visit a preschool or kindergarten class. Challenge your class to make these plans with a church or school that has a substantial number of low-income or needy children. Plan for your groups to ask follow-up questions to encourage the children to discuss the biblical value of the book.

Your class can also make copies of the book for the children. A copy center will scan, print, and collate the books. The books can then be bound with brass brads. As one person in a group reads the story to the children, the other group members can hand out copies and write the children's names on the books.

Later, gather your groups together to pray that these children have learned the message from God's Word.

REACHING *Out* TO *Others*

HOW TO TREAT A NEIGHBOR

Overview: Group members will make and deliver treats to someone who could use a friendly gesture.

Supplies: Equipment and ingredients for making the treat your group chooses.

Activity:

Plan this activity a week or two in advance. Begin by having each participant (or couple) identify at least one non-Christian person or family in his or her neighborhood who would appreciate a friendly gesture. Then plan what kind of cookies or treats your group will make to deliver to those people. You might make it something seasonal, something fancy, or something plain. Do whichever your group feels would have the most positive effect on the people receiving the treats.

Assign ingredients for people to bring, and be sure to specify amounts. At the time of your meeting, work together to make, bake, and package the treats. Also during that time, have people write notes to go with the treats. Encourage group members to refrain from getting preachy in their notes, but to make it clear that the treat is being given because the group member cares about that person or family. If a computer with the right software is available, people may be able to design and print customized cards. If time allows, have each participant or couple deliver the treat the same evening. If possible, meet together afterward to discuss the following questions.

- **How did the people respond when you delivered the treats?**

- **How do you think the kind gesture affected their opinions of you?**

- **What might this gesture do in laying the groundwork for possibly sharing your faith sometime in the future?**

- **What are some good ways to start conversations about faith with non-Christians?**

REACHING *Out* **TO** *Others*

FAITH IN ACTION

Overview: Group members will look at a passage of Scripture about putting faith into action, and then choose a service project to do together.

Supplies: You'll need Bibles.

Activity:

Begin this activity by having every person in your group tell what having faith in Christ means in their lives. Then have someone read aloud James 2:14-17. Discuss the following questions in your group:

- **What does this passage say about the importance of demonstrating our faith in our actions?**
- **What does this passage say about our responsibility to help others who are in need?**
- **How can we be more sensitive to those in need around us?**

Have your group consider what you might take on as a one-time or an ongoing service or outreach project. Here are some possibilities:

- Take on support of a child through Compassion International.
- Collect food for a local agency that distributes food to hungry people.
- Volunteer at a local agency that helps needy people.
- Raise support in the community or workplaces for agencies that help homeless people.
- Start or work in a program in your church that assists needy people.
- Give regularly to agencies helping people around the world, such as World Vision.
- Together, skip a meal on a regular basis and donate the money you would have spent on that meal to feeding hungry people.
- Covenant together to call each other and take action when one of you comes in contact with someone in real need.

When group members have chosen an activity, have them each take particular responsibilities in making sure the group follows through on what it's chosen to do. Help your group set dates to start and plan to get the project going as soon as possible.

REACHING *Out* TO *Others*

MEALTIME MEMORIES

Overview: Group members will spend time getting to know one or more senior adults, record their memories of a favorite meal, and plan meals to share with them.

Supplies: You'll need one tape recorder for each senior adult interviewed, a camera, photo album, and food supplies for the planned meal.

Activity:

Before the meeting, choose one or more senior adults to interview. Preferably, find people who don't have family nearby. Speak to someone at your church, in your group, or at an assisted-living home in order to find individuals who would be interested in talking to the group. Likewise, make sure they can attend a meal later on. When you've chosen your senior adults, provide one tape player for each.

When group members arrive, begin a discussion about favorite meals. Ask group members what they prefer for their favorite meal. Next, talk about how people seem to use mealtimes as opportunities to build relationships. Perhaps people can share about mealtimes they spent as children with their families or what they do at mealtimes today.

Tell your group how they can use the mealtime as an opportunity to reach out to others. Introduce the names of each of your senior adults and explain to the group the details of your outreach activity. Form groups of two or more, and have each group take a tape player and visit one of the senior adults. Have group members spend time talking to the senior adults and getting to know them. At some point in the conversation, have group members ask the senior adult to describe his or her favorite meal. Record the conversations, and make sure the senior adults explain exactly what their favorite meals include.

As a group, come back together and plan a special meal for each of the senior adults and your group. Send the seniors a special invitation and plan for someone to pick them up for the meal. Plan a meal for each senior adult according to his or her memories. It could be formal, casual, or even a picnic.

During the meals, group members should spend time listening to their guests talk about the memories the meal brings to them. Make sure to take several photographs of each senior adult enjoying a meal with people from your group. After the pictures are developed, have the group put together a small photo album for the senior adult with pictures and some encouraging notes. Be sure to identify each person in the photos and create a title page to help the senior adult remember the date and event. You might even find your group wants to adopt the senior adult as a "grandparent."

*Wow*Tip

Your group may find that they can do more than just fix a meal for its senior adults. Your outreach activity could expand to helping them out in several different ways, from taking them shopping to spending time with them where they live.

REACHING *Out* TO *Others*